MW01199720

"This book might be (Daelemans's *An Ignat* uplifting and interestii ....plating the Way of the Cross through poetic writing, visual images, and selected pieces of music in the context of the Ignatian tradition. For those who seek beauty, hope, and inspiration, the book will be a source of reflection and sustenance."

—Gesa Thiessen, Trinity College, Dublin, Ireland

"St. Ignatius of Loyola's *Spiritual Exercises* have formed the basis of numerous retreats and meditations across the centuries since they were first completed in 1541. He proposed that as a reader one 'represent to yourself in the imagination' the scene being described, and in this short volume Bert Daelemans takes him at his word by centering his own meditations around the work of the contemporary German sculptor, Werner Klenk (b. 1942). Daelemans already has in print a profound analysis of how modern architecture and the contemporary church might successfully interact. Here he displays equal insight into some of the other arts but in a way that never loses sight of overarching pastoral and spiritual concerns."

—David Brown
   Wardlaw Professor of Theology, Aesthetics and Culture
   University of St Andrews, Fellow of the British Academy

"More than mere devotional practice, this contemporary, existential, and artistic Way of the Cross is at once a guide to meditation and a path to encounter Christ in whom we are and find what we are searching for: a fullness of joy and life beyond our own darkness and our daily struggles."

—Georges Ruyssen, SJ
   Pontificio Istituto Orientale, Rome, Italy

"Bert Daelemans, SJ, gently guides us in the contemplation of the Passion of Jesus through a series of sculptural images. As we, reverently or even shyly, approach Jesus in this *via crucis*, we are led to discover that it is Jesus who walks with us during the course of our lives. We are captivated by Jesus in these most genuinely human moments of his divinity—to see, to listen, to feel, and even to taste the beauty, the truth, and the proximity of God living and embracing our humanity. By way of a dialogue with this Jesus, so truly meek and humble, we are encouraged to experience a moving encounter with him in a journey of discernment so as to grow in his likeness."

—Miyako Namikawa, RSCJ, Madrid, Spain

"Fr. Daelemans's sensitive interpretation of the Ignatian text, enhanced by Werner Klenk's beautifully photographed Way of the Cross in bronze, offers an engaging and deeply personal spiritual experience. In this relatively compact work, the full range of our human capacities for prayer—imagination, the senses, memory, and intuition—are brought into play. We move at our own pace. The graced moments ripen slowly. This is a book to keep."

—Fr. William Pearsall, SJ
University Chaplain, University of Manchester

"This is a wonderful book, which invites us on a journey with Jesus as he faces his most difficult and most glorious moments on his journey of the Cross. It is a tough and challenging journey—almost harrowing, yet intimate and beautiful—calling us to explore the depth of our own being and all of our relationships, not least with Jesus and with ourselves. This is a text I have and will use often for meditation and contemplation, and I found the use of images and music suggestions, along with the Scripture and almost poetic text, really helpful and evocative—drawing me into the exercises in spite of my reluctance!"

—Jim Culliton, SJ, Dublin, Ireland

"For anyone seeking to walk with Christ in the dynamic of the Exercises and willing to allow Christ's Passion to meld with her or his own struggles, hopes, and desires, this is a book one can savor and keep exploring for its many doorways into the Christian Mystery we believe and live. It is ideal for individuals, spiritual directors who companion contemporary pilgrims, and community prayer groups choosing Christ together. He bids us to 'breathe in' the grace of each movement and to 'breathe out' a response, offered as a gift. This is an integrated Catholic spirituality in its fullest expression and depth."

—Paul A. Janowiak, SJ
Jesuit School of Theology of Santa Clara University

"It is rare to find a spiritual writer who combines so many gifts: theology, aesthetics, and intimate familiarity with Saint Ignatius's wisdom about prayer. An Ignatian Journey combines art, Scripture, poetry, and even suggestions for music in a single, multifaceted meditation. As with Saint Ignatius's great classic, the Spiritual Exercises, the prayer engages the senses, the imagination, and the heart. I am sure that any who desire a deeper and more personal encounter with the Lord will find in this unusual and beautiful book a continual source of inspiration."

—Nicholas Austin, SJ, Heythrop College

An Ignatian Journey of the Cross

Exercises in Discernment

Bert Daelemans, SJ

Foreword by

Jane Ferdon, OP,
and George R. Murphy, SJ

LITURGICAL PRESS
Collegeville, Minnesota

www.litpress.org

Scripture texts in this work are taken from the New Revised Standard Version Bible, © 1989, Division of Christian Education of the National Council of the Churches of Christ in the United States of America. Used by permission. All rights reserved.

1   2   3   4   5   6   7   8   9

Library of Congress Cataloging-in-Publication Data

Daelemans, Bert.
    An Ignatian journey of the cross : exercises in discernment /
Bert Daelemans, S.J.
        pages cm
    ISBN 978-0-8146-4718-9 — ISBN 978-0-8146-4743-1 (ebook)
    1. Ignatius, of Loyola, Saint, 1491–1556. Exercitia spiritualia.
    2. Spiritual life—Catholic Church.   3. Spiritual exercises.   I. Title.

BX2179.L8D34   2015
232.96—dc23   2015025004

Dans nos ténèbres, il n'y a pas une place pour la Beauté.
Toute la place est pour la Beauté.

In our darkness, there is no place for beauty.
Beauty fills all space.

René Char (1907–1988)

To Aylan (+2015)

Contents

A golden rule . . .

We ought to note well the course of the thoughts,

And if the beginning, middle, and end is all good, inclined to all good,

It is a sign of the good Angel;

But if in the course of the thoughts which he brings it ends in something bad,

Of a distracting tendency, or less good than what the soul had previously proposed to do,

Or if it weakens it or disquiets or disturbs the soul,

Taking away its peace, tranquility and quiet, which it had before,

It is a clear sign that it proceeds from the evil spirit, enemy of our profit and eternal salvation. [SpEx 333]

Foreword

Artists feed each other in their search for beauty and truth. This book, for seekers of truth and beauty, for believers and unbelievers, invites us into a variety of encounters across time on what it means to be human: the sculpture of German artist Werner Klenk; the art of photography; a series of classical musicians; the Christian and Hebrew Scriptures; the prayers, reflections, questions, and insights of a person schooled in Ignatian spirituality and Christian humanism. It is an eminently contemplative book at the interface of seeing and hearing, thinking and feeling, remembering and hoping.

When contemplation, according to the eminent preacher Walter Burghardt, is defined as "a long, loving look at the real," one might anticipate beautiful sunrises, magnificent clouds, breathtaking horizons or other heartwarming scenes. Daelemans's book does not fulfill that kind of anticipation. He sees "the real" but it is the real that confronts suffering and brings out a beauty and intimacy that can be found there. Daelemans reflects on the Way of the Cross and the Jesus who reveals himself there.

Ecce homo—behold the man. This is not, at first glance, the triumphant King, the victorious warrior. This is the condemned person, beaten, scourged, humiliated, judged worthy of the death penalty. He is not the energetic, youthful preacher and healer who attracts large crowds of enthusiastic followers. Nevertheless, Daelemans brings us into an encounter with a beautiful man, the tragedy of love abandoned, betrayed, rejected, but the beauty of faithful love, the beauty of encountering help along the way, the beauty of courageous endurance.

The book is subtitled "discernment." This is the discernment necessary in times of darkness and suffering. Is this a darkness where the Holy One invites us or the invitation of a destructive spirit? Is the darkness a desolation, leading us away from God and the Holy and the human, or is the darkness a consoling invitation to intimacy, to friendship in difficult times, to help and accompaniment, to courageous endurance and acceptance?

This book compels us to stop along the way, to engage a very human Jesus, to let surface our deepest fears, longings, and hopes. We meet a Jesus who falls, who needs help and receives it from strangers, from friends, and from family, who consoles others and is not blind to their suffering even as he suffers. This Jesus knows the pain of suffering, loneliness, betrayal, disappointment, and failure. He also knows the fidelity of a God who sustains him.

Daelemans, like the Way of the Cross, does not romanticize suffering, nor does he deny it. In facing his way, Jesus opens the way for us. Daelemans is a trustworthy and knowledgeable companion. Savor the book, savor the journey.

Jane Ferdon, OP, and George R. Murphy, SJ

Before You Go This Way

Pathfinders are pathseekers who keep walking
because they know where to find traces of the way.

Godfinders are Godseekers who keep walking
because they know where to find faces of God.

This book is a collection of fifteen spiritual exercises for people who search to experience God with the help of Ignatian discernment. This Ignatian journey helps to discover clues in discernment by contemplating Christ in his Passion. It is written in such a way as to foster the integration of Ignatian spirituality with everyday life. By contemplating a work of art, we are invited to follow step by step the downward path of the disfigured Christ who configures us in his glorious transfiguration. We all share his humanity: let us also share his divinity, the glory of his cross.

Art and beauty have long been able to deepen our spirituality. The Ignatian journey indicated here follows the steadfast rhythm of a bronze Way of the Cross, by German artist Werner Klenk. In this beautiful artwork, he has captured with astonishing and disarming power the essence of a Christian lifestyle made of encounters. Most of the time, we tend to look at art from a purely aesthetic point of view. We do not always have the clues to release the theological depth that is often hidden in the greatest masterpieces. This is one intention of this book: to guide us in the fascinating discovery of the Christian Mystery present in a work of art. This is already an Ignatian journey that connects us with our senses, imagination, and memory.

The second aim is to show the true extension of the Passion of Christ as depicted in a Way of the Cross. Most of the time, a *via crucis* is reduced to a popular form of religious piety. This goes beyond the extraordinary power of the *via crucis* to shed light on everyday life—often disgracefully touched by the cross in all its forms. The nearness of Christ in this masterpiece of Werner Klenk is disarmingly and powerfully palpable even on a photograph.

The third aim is to go this Way of the Cross as an Ignatian journey of discernment. Remarkably, the rules of discernment of the Spiritual Exercises can easily be pointed out in this Way of the Cross, which is made essentially of encounters between persons.

At times, life looks like a Way of the Cross. Pain is there, uninvited. It seems impossible to discern the smallest source of light in the tremendous darkness that surrounds us. Fortunately, nobody walks this way alone. This little guide is a practical introduction in Ignatian discernment, retrieving the old tradition of including imagery for prayer purposes.

Each station is a different spiritual exercise for growing in divinely human values, such as humility, solidarity, tenderness, etc. Together, they reveal the magnificent vulnerability of our shared humanity and the glorious miracle of our shared divinity. No prerequisites are needed for this book: only the willingness to contemplate, to recognize, and to savor what makes us profoundly human will reveal the disarming, nascent beauty that our world secretly longs for.

The slow and silent contemplation of this work of art gave way to a series of spiritual exercises in the tradition of St. Ignatius of Loyola. In the four steps that I propose here, you will easily recognize the well-known Ignatian pattern of the Four Weeks. At the end of each step, you might go back to the exercises offered here, so as to collect and revisit the moments of grace when you savored more fruit and profit.

> For it is not knowing much, but realizing and relishing
>   things interiorly,
> That contents and satisfies the soul. [SpEx 2]

The emphasis of these spiritual exercises lies on the attentive contemplation of the sculpture and the mystery it brings to light. Bronze communicates so much more than words alone can tell. Often, not only during Lent, our life resembles a Way of the Cross. When many voices obscure our way, it will be essential to discern the encounters that give life:

> Therefore they have need to be very well examined
> Before entire credit is given them, or they are put into
>   effect. [SpEx 336]

Before each exercise, I suggest some biblical readings, a passage of the Ignatian Spiritual Exercises, and a piece of music, which all might help to release more of the mystery enclosed in the encounter between universal truth and your particular daily life. An easy rule to discern God is this:

> It is proper to God [. . .] to give true spiritual gladness
>   and joy,
> Taking away all sadness and disturbance. [SpEx 329]

The text is intended to make easier this contemplative act. Word and image belong together in order to make room for our own mystery. At times, we will feel the need to stop reading so that deeper echoes may come to the surface. The dialogue between text and image brings to light the centrality of the cross in Jesus' life and in our own lives:

> If any want to become my followers,
> Let them [. . .] take up their cross daily and follow me.
>   (Luke 9:23)

The Way of the Cross (1987–1988) from the German artist Werner Klenk (www.klenk-bildhauer.de) can be admired in the church of Maria Königin in Lennestadt, Germany. This work consists of three reliefs (50x250) in bronze, each depicting five Stations of the Cross.

The Spiritual Exercises of St. Ignatius of Loyola are quoted according to the translation of Elder Mullan, SJ (1914) [SpEx].

Photography: Rudolf Paulus (†) and Bert Daelemans, SJ

My profound gratitude is due to John Dardis, SJ, for proofreading this text.

FIRST STEP

WORLD—THREE ATTITUDES

The first step consists in contemplating three basic attitudes of Christ in relation to our world, in order to kindle my desire to follow him in this world.

MAKING A CHOICE   HERE I AM   HUMILITY

In this first step, it helps to savor the contrast between the attitudes of Christ and the indifference, hedonism, or violence of our present world and to discover within this world an immense, albeit at times fragile, desire for peace and communion.

> Consider how Christ our Lord puts himself [. . .]
> In a lowly place, beautiful and attractive. [SpEx 144]

1

MAKING A CHOICE

Ecce homo: Jesus or Pilate?

The good Angel touches [. . .] sweetly, lightly, and gently,
Like a drop of water which enters into a sponge;
And the evil touches [. . .] sharply and with noise and disquiet,
As when the drop of water falls on stone. [SpEx 335]

READINGS: Ps 40; John 19:1-16; Matt 27:15-26
EXERCISES: Meditation on the two standards [SpEx 136–147]
MUSIC: Johann Sebastian Bach (1685–1750), *O Haupt voll Blut und Wunden*, from *Matthäus Passion*

Here is the man! (John 19:5)

Thus starts our story with Jesus.
Someone has shown us this man.
Here is that other man, Pilate.

A man rises out of the bronze.
Another seems to become bronze.
He stands still, dreadfully alone.
Even though the other one looks at Him.
Alone—precisely because the other one
Looks down at him.

There is no greater contrast than this:

One high on his throne,
The other stands at his feet;

One comfortably inside,
The other in the cold outside;

One protected,
The other projected;

One richly clothed,
The other indefensibly naked;

One without face,
The other pure expression;

Hands that are cramped and closed,
Hands that are open, free, and innocent.

One washes his hands in guilt,
The other cleansed the feet of his friends;

One anonymously in his own name,
The other in name of God and—quite simply—of everyone;

One apparently free
But, in fact, brutally imprisoned
The other detained
And entirely free;

The one as slave
The other as king.

Smashed in a corner,
Thirty silver coins sadly
Witness the bloody treason
Of the disciple, the friend, the other who left him, who
   cut himself out.

    Here is the man!

I recognize myself in the metallic mask of the one
And in the vulnerable gaze of the other.

I know: behind this opaque superficiality
I also hide with my harsh judgment.
This is me.

   . . . the water in the dish has dried up.

Two deep, gentle eyes look at me.
I recognize this pain.
Vulnerability looks at me
In this searching gaze: my own
And that of my neighbor.

Only in this inquiring gaze
Will we drink Living Water.

Only in this most refined and personal center
Do I find depth and rest.

Only in this helpless and consoling gaze
That approaches me
And adopts all human cries
Does God give Godself away
And do I find an answer.

    Here is the man!

It is good to see God in this man.
Good to see how to be human.

It is good to lift up our eyes to this human being,
Like Adam and Eve, like desert people
Lifting up their eyes to the serpent (Gen 2:4–3:24;
    Num 21:4; John 3:14).

"Behold the man" is first of all
Daring to look at humanity,
My being human.

"Behold the Man" is also
Daring to look at sinfulness,
Not in an oppressing way,
But in an uplifting way,
Taking me as I am.

To look is to lift up the eyes,
Not looking down and not moving anymore,
What is always the easiest way.

This looking is a lifting and a longing
To Someone who has seen me long before I opened my
    eyes.

    To behold this human being
    Is to encounter God.

This is the judgment of Pilate:
Not only does he condemn Christ,
But also himself.

Every time that we judge the other,
We sharply judge ourselves.

Behold the man,
The broken, humiliated man.

He was detained in the night,
Betrayed by a kiss,
Mocked even though He was innocent,
Beaten up and handed over.

Behold the broken Body
And dare to see God.

Behold the broken Bread
And see Life.

When all are scattered,
Jesus teaches us with His Body.

When He is going to die, alone,
Jesus teaches us with His Body.

He gives away his Body
So that we become his Body.

His Body washes the feet of Simon
And receives the kiss of Judas.

On the moment of separation,
Jesus teaches us with the intimacy of his Body.

Instead of separation,
Jesus says: intimacy.

Instead of brokenness,
Jesus sings: communion.

He does not take away the separation and the brokenness,
But speaks with silent words that everybody understands
And dances on the rhythm of a very old tune that we all
   know.

> Here is the Lamb of God
> Who takes away the sins of the world! (John 1:29)

Such was the Epiphany—revelation—of the Baptist.

> Here is the man! (John 19:5)

Such is the Epiphany of the coward

. . . that I am.

Cowards cannot condemn him.
Closed, accomplice hands: you cannot come to me.
The one hand hides the other.

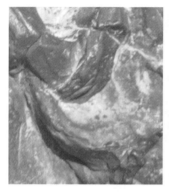 

Jesus, instead, gives himself
With open, patient hands:
Here I am. Compliant, serene.

This man is abandoned,
Left alone.

Ah, why did they not leave him alone!

No, harsh words make him small.
The tough gaze of Pilate: *Here is the man!*
The stiff silence, the traitor's kiss of Judas.
The hard judgment of the people: *Crucify him!* (John 19:15)
My rigid look: this human nonbeing cannot be God.

His answer?

A pure and silent

YES

To life,
To love,
To God,
To humanity:

Foundation of his life,
The YES that he is and wants to be, now and forever.

Behold the Bridegroom.

He stands in our midst
As the one who serves (Luke 22:27),
And washes our feet (John 13:5).

Behold the King.
There are two kings in front
of us:
The faceless king on his
throne
And the broken king with the
crown of thorns
In the midst of a crowd of
thorns.

. . . whom will I follow?

During a few contemplative moments,
I pray, let go . . .

Breathing in: *This is my Son . . .*
Breathing out: *. . . listen to him.* (Matt 17:5)

God,
Bound hand and foot in Your Son,
Surrendered due to our arbitrariness,
Also today You give Yourself as the True Way to Life.

Awaken in us Your Spirit so that,
From now on, we do not judge but console.

2

HERE I AM

Jesus accepts his cross

It is proper to the evil Angel [. . .] under the appearance of an
angel of light,
[. . .] to bring good and holy thoughts. [SpEx 332]

READINGS: Mark 8:34-37; Matt 11:29-30; Phil 2:8
EXERCISES: Contemplation of the Incarnation [SpEx 101–109]
MUSIC: Georg Frideric Händel (1685–1759), *Vouchsafe,* from *Utrecht
Te Deum*

Out of nowhere, a burden, a wooden beam.
A heavy load, that is all.
A tough, rough resistance.

A severe, rolling wind.
An adversary impossible to overcome.

This is bad! says the angel of light.
Don't go this way!

Jesus accepts this burden.
He takes it upon his shoulders.

He pushes this burden forward,
Upward, with steadfast gaze
As a solid, resisting rock.
A strong man. A carpenter's son.

Such determination is not born out of his own power
But out of an inner strength, that he knows to find in the
  deep.

  My yoke is easy and my burden is light. (Matt 11:30)

A yoke serves to make the burden easier to carry.

The burden seems to fall upon him from above.
Resolutely he answers from the deep,
Out of a fragility that is his force (2 Cor 12:10)
And whose name is Abba.

His gaze is fragile enough to break through the burden.
He shines through all our burdens.
His gaze rests upon women, children, and men
Who have to carry such a burden. Today.

And resolutely he carries their burden.

This burden is not only his.
It is the unbearable resistance of our world.

It is everything that resists,
           refuses,
           refutes,
           defies,
           opposes,
           counters,
           blocks
What I am called to do
Who we are called to be.

A man takes a burden upon his shoulders.
A brief moment with long-lasting effect.

In contrast to the first, static and magnificent station
This one rises up as an overwhelming wave out of a sea
     of bronze
One solidified gesture of pure humanity.

After Pilate had showed Christ shamelessly in his naked
     passion,
Now we see him fully clothed in action.

It is impossible to carry such a burden.
No human being can possibly do that.

> Behold the Lamb of God,
>   who takes away the sin of the world! (John 1:29)

Jesus accepted. He agreed. He took our burdens upon him.
He received. He consented. He said yes. Again and again.

Behold the Man, who resolutely accepts his mission.
He accepts his cross.
He takes up his cross, daily. (Luke 9:23)

This cross is also the log in my eye
That blinds me to see the speck in my brother's eye.
   (Matt 7:3)

This cross is also my resistance
That refuses life to love easily.

Carrying this cross
Jesus transposes log into love.

This cross, carrying him soon enough
Will be transposed into tree of life.

The Lamb of God takes up the lost lamb
And lays it on his shoulders
And rejoices. (Luke 15:5)

It's me, this lamb.
It's the Church, weak and vulnerable.

During a few contemplative moments,
I pray, let go . . .

> Breathing in: *Here I am . . .*
> Breathing out: *. . . to do your will.* (Ps 40:7-8)

God,
Vulnerably hidden in Your Son,
Overpowered by our resistance,
Also today You reveal Yourself
As inexhaustible depth and strength.

Awaken in us Your Spirit so that,
From now on, we do not resist,
But resolutely accept our cross.

3

HUMILITY
Jesus falls

In times of desolation never to make a change;
But be firm and constant. [SpEx 318]

READINGS: Ps 13; Lam 1; John 8:6-11
EXERCISES: Meditation on my own sins [SpEx 55–61]
MUSIC: Gabriel Fauré (1845–1924), *Pie Jesu*, from *Requiem*

Here is the man . . .

Crushed. Fallen. In pain.
Small. A nobody.

Though he was in the form of God
He did not regard equality with God
As something to be exploited
But emptied himself. (Phil 2:6-7)

My Savior has fallen.
My Savior is crushed.

> How would we drink his Blood
> If Christ had not been crushed?
>
> How would we share his Cup
> If Christ had not accepted it? (St. Cyprian)

The cross of sins pushes him towards the ground.
From there he watches the world:
From the eye-level of children and beggars.
Our strange, crazy world.

Actually, he is already standing up.

He kneels.

Just like then,
Writing in the
    soft dust.
Next to him, a
    woman.
Standing.
    Accused.

Neither do I condemn you.
Go your way, and from now on do not sin again.
    (John 8:11)

That's God's judgment.
So different than ours.

    Crucify him! Crucify him! (Luke 23:21)

He emptied himself.
Not we.
So full of ourselves.

He must increase, but I must decrease. (John 3:30)

Real greatness
Knows how to become small.
Sin proves its nothingness
By its constant need to prove itself.

He kneels.

Just like then,
Washing the feet of his friends.
Next to him, Peter.
Standing. Refusing.

Unless I wash you, you have no share with me. (John 13:8)

That's God's invitation.
So different than ours.

God looks up at us.
God reveals God's self from below.
God reverses our logic and expectations.

Only such a face
Can heal me from within,
Get me whole again,
Make me myself again.
Image and likeness of God (Gen 1:26).
Unique child of God.

He kneels.

Just like then,
On the Mount of Olives (Luke 22:40).

Alone.

His closest friends are sleeping.
Dreaming of a better world.
Or winning imaginary battles.
And healing incurable diseases.

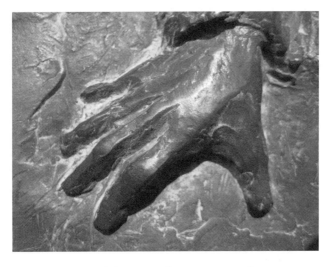

In his anguish he prayed more earnestly,
and his sweat became like drops of blood falling down
on the ground. (Luke 22:44)

With one hand, he pushes himself up.
He stands again, resolutely.
He embraces his cross.
It rubs his cheek,
The one that Judas kissed,
A minute ago.

He lifts his cross,
The wound of the world,
Like the Lamb of God
Carrying the lost sheep.

Eyes wide open.
   Still looking at the suffering world in front of him.
   He does not carry his pain.
   He carries our pain.
His mouth stuck in a cry.

Still murmuring consoling words.
He does not break himself off from this world.
He is there, where you are suffering.
His face torn in inhuman effort.

Here is the man!

Can you believe it?
This is God!
This is our Savior!
What a bizarre way to save the world!
Our King . . . a humiliated nobody!

Whoever has seen me has seen the Father. (John 14:9)

During a few contemplative moments,
I pray, let go . . .

Breathing in:　*Though he was rich . . .*
Breathing out:　*. . . for us he became poor.* (2 Cor 8:9)

*God,
Crushed to the earth in Your Son,
Bent under our sins,
Also today You labor in our world
So that we are lifted up.*

*Awaken in us Your Spirit so that,
From now on, we do not pretend to be great
But become smaller.*

SECOND STEP

MISSION—FIVE ENCOUNTERS

In this second step, I contemplate the mission of Jesus as narrated in five basic encounters. His mission is defined through his encounters—with women, men, children, his mother, his Father, his friends, his disciples, and us. Here are five spiritual exercises in order to exercise my capacity for tenderness, solidarity, gratuity, fidelity, and consolation. I let these resonate in me. It is a mission! I let myself be defined, conformed, modeled by these encounters and take profit from my contemplations. Could this also be my mission?

You, follow me. (John 21:22)

TENDERNESS

SOLIDARITY

GRATUITY

FIDELITY

CONSOLATION

To ask for interior knowledge of the Lord,

Who for me has become man,

That I may more love and follow him.
[SpEx 104]

LEIT
LIEB

MENSCHENSOHN

4

TENDERNESS
Jesus meets his mother

Love ought to be put more in deeds than in words. [SpEx 230]

READINGS: Luke 2:22-35; John 19:25-27
EXERCISES: Contemplation of the Nativity [SpEx 110–117]
MUSIC: Johann Sebastian Bach (1685–1750), *Ich will dir mein Herze schenken*, from *Matthäus Passion*

Only love is alive.

A first encounter on the way.
A strange encounter: Jesus is not free.

The burden is heavy. It hurts.
However, the unbearable cannot impede him
From encountering tenderness.

His mother breaks through all the defenses
And causes the Way of the Cross to stop.
For a short time. A brief moment of eternity.
The Way of the Cross holds its breath.

A kiss.
So different from Judas!
Then, the kiss humiliated him.
Now, the kiss humanizes him.

A kiss so pure, with tenderness and love.
This is the last kiss that will be given to the Son of Man.
This kiss is Mary's last word.
This is all she has to say.

I love you, my son.
I go with you.
Never forget that.
I bless you.
Go, in the peace of the Lord!

Jesus cannot even answer her.
He can only accept, agree, receive.

He does not resist.
He does not protect himself
From unbearable love.
No love is unbearable to him.

He accepts every form of love.
Every form.

Gently, he bows his knees
Under the burden of our sins.

Gently, he bows his knees
To receive the kiss of his mother.

He is entirely turned towards her.
With a kiss, she humanizes the humiliation.

In the midst of the street,
In the midst of the noise.

But they have no ears for that noise and these insults.
For a brief moment,
They have only ears and eyes
For this love that passes through them,
This Holy Spirit,
This breath of life.

With her left hand—hand of her heart
She gently slides around
The face of her son—son of her heart.

Her hand as a small shell at his ear.
Can you hear the sea?
Do you remember that day?
Will you dream with me?

Strong, vigorous, that hand,
The hand of a mother.
Their hands touch barely.

He carries the burden of the world.
She carries him, for a moment of eternity.

Gently, she turns him towards her.
It is as if she whispers a last word in his ear.
Words that we do not have to hear.
Words that we do not have to understand.
Intimate words of lovers.

He's a listener.
For a brief moment, he forgets the burden.
He is totally hers now.
He is totally given,
Surrendered to this fragile instant of love.
His gaze is where she is.

Heaven and earth meet here.

The mother of God whispers here the Word.

Robustly, with her right hand, she lifts the burden,
Strong mother of the carpenter's son.
For a moment, it even seems his arm,
But no, it is definitely hers.

She frees space to encrust, insert, incorporate herself,
To be tenderness,

To be close to his heart,
To hearten him.

Now they both carry the cross.

Resolutely, she takes her place.
The place she deserves.
The place she chooses.
The place next to her son:
Strong, resilient, standing.

A column, a support, a caryatid.

And then: she lets him go.

Love is her open secret.
Love is her revealed agenda.
Love is her last word.

During a few contemplative moments,
I pray, let go . . .

Breathing in: *Let it be with me . . .*
Breathing out: *. . . according to your word.* (Luke 1:38)

> *God,*
> *Hidden Abba in Your humiliated Son,*
> *Resolute tenderness in His Mother,*
> *Also today You want to be encounter*
> *In the midst of desolation.*
>
> *Awaken in us Your Spirit so that,*
> *From now on, we do not shield ourselves*
> *But allow ourselves to be loved.*

5

SOLIDARITY

Jesus meets Simon

It is proper to the good spirit to give courage and strength,
Consolations, tears, inspirations and quiet,
Easing, and putting away all obstacles,
That one may go on in well doing. [SpEx 315]

> READINGS: Matt 26:31-35, 69-75; 27:27-44
> EXERCISES: Meditation of the three persons [SpEx 149–157]
> MUSIC: Antonio Caldara (1670–1736), *O fortunate lacrime*, from
> *Maddalena ai piedi di Cristo*

> As they went out, they came upon a man from Cyrene
>   named Simon;
> They compelled this man to carry his cross. (Matt 27:32)

A new, unforeseen encounter on the Way of the Cross.
He emerges out of nowhere, this complete stranger.
Out of bronze: two strong hands and a face.
Like a very human *deus ex machina.*
He does not remain safely at the side.
He does not stay in the dark.
He steps forward, into the light.

Here I am.

Into the Light of the world.

Chosen to be Jesus' helper.
Compelled to be his companion.
Cut out of the multitude.

You are the one.

The soldiers force him to follow Jesus,
To be his follower and friend.

This *deus ex machina* will not resolve everything.
He won't resolve anything at all.
He will only be there, next to his Lord,
In his shirtsleeves like the carpenter's son:
Alter Christus.

He suits the action to the word,
To the Word of God.

Simon does not choose the cross.
It is already there.
Without a word,
He lifts it upon his shoulder.

What a relief for Christ!

Grateful, Christ turns around
And lifts his gaze upon Simon.
He shows him the face of the Father.
Only God can look like that: up and back at a human being.

Jesus' eyes rest upon him.
Just like the other day, with the searching young man:

> Jesus, looking at him, loved him and said:
> "You lack one thing; go, sell what you own,
> and give the money to the poor,
> and you will have treasure in heaven;
> then come, follow me." (Mark 10:21)

Perhaps Simon is this rich man
Who came back to follow him.
Perhaps it is not him.
In any case, Jesus takes time
To broaden any brief instant to unforgettable eternity.

Jesus looks back and calls him:
"Simon, do you really want to follow me?"

Carrying the cross, Simon will become Jesus' closest friend.
Carrying the cross, Simon will become Christian.

The burden that they both carry
Will become their strongest bond.

Their arms cross.
The cross brings them together.
This cross shapes Simon into another Christ,
Into a Christian.

Silently, they look at each other.
The one is reflected in the other.
The one rests in the other.
They do not need words.
They understand.
Their eyes speak,
Their hands embrace,
Their hearts beat the same rhythm.

Totally absent from this Way of the Cross is
The other Simon, also named Peter the Rock,
The one on which Jesus had built his Church (Matt 16:18)
But who had said: My religion has no cross! (Matt 16:22)
And: I will do everything for you,
But you, do not touch me! (John 13:8).

In the shadow of the Light
And in the silence of the Word
He is going his own way of the Cross.

Also to him Jesus had turned his face,
But he had said:

   I do not know the man! (Matt 26:74)

The Rock has still to be washed in tears of bitterness
In order to be new, able to carry a Church.

> Unless I wash you, you have no share with me. (John 13:8)

Also there, the kneeling Jesus has looked up at him
And had called him:
"Simon, do you really want to follow me?"

Finally, Peter understands.

> A man had two sons.

To both of them he said:

> "Son, go and work in the vineyard today."

The first, Simon Peter, answered:

> "I go, sir."
> But he did not go.

The other, Simon of Cyrene, answered:

> "I will not."
> But later he changed his mind and went. (Matt 21:28-30)

I recognize both dynamics in me.
When everything goes fine,
I eagerly take up my cross.

But he did not go.

When everything goes wrong,
It is precisely my cross that becomes my love.

But later he changed his mind and went.

From now on, for the rest of his life,
Jesus will not walk alone.
Simon follows him, faithful and hidden,
Adopting his unlikely rhythm.
We will not hear from him anymore.
But he is there, in the shadow of his Lord.
During a few contemplative moments,
I pray, let go . . .

Breathing in: *Let the light of your face . . .*
Breathing out: *. . . shine on us, O Lord.* (Ps 4:6)

God,
Inexhaustible source of love in Your Son,
Forgotten by our world,
Also today You light up your Face.

Awaken in us Your Spirit
So that, from now on, we do not observe from afar
But hasten to help, even though we do not know where
this will lead us.

6

GRATUITY
Jesus meets Veronica

I call consolation every increase of hope, faith, and charity.
[SpEx 316]

. . . even the smallest one.

READINGS: Isa 53:2-5; Matt 25:31-46; Matt 26:6-13; Isa 53:2-5
EXERCISES: To save the proposition of the other [SpEx 22]
MUSIC: Antonio Caldara (1670–1736), *Spera consolati*, from
Maddalena ai piedi di Cristo

Here is the man . . .

. . . with shaky knees.
Helped by a woman,
Greater than him.
Strong, as a tree giving him
Shadow, refreshment, Spirit.
He bows himself towards her outstretched hand
In everlasting offering.

She inclines herself towards him:
Deaconess, good Samaritan, divine woman.

> Whoever gives you a cup of water to drink
> Because you bear the name of Christ
> Will by no means lose the reward. (Mark 9:21)

Wise, creative Veronica!
You do not compare yourself with Simon
Or with Mary the Mother of God.
You find your own way
To be encounter on the way.
It is not much,
It is all she gives.
It is all she has.

> She out of her poverty has put in
> All she had to live on. (Luke 21:4)

She gives herself.
Like he does.
Look at him!

They do not talk.
They do not look each other in the face.
Their encounter is deeper,
On the level of the heart.

There, at his heart,
Where she holds her hand,
There they look at each other,
There the Lord lets his face shine on her. (Ps 4:6)

There, at his heart,
Is she the *vera icon*,
True image and resemblance of God. (Gen 1:26)

There, at his sacred heart,
Is she mirrored in Jesus' face.
Is he imprinted on her cloth, in her hand.

There, at his sacred heart,
She acknowledges her priesthood.

Her right foot is gently displaced
As if she were dancing.
A brief moment of service and glory.

In this bloody, mistreated face
Of a complete stranger
She recognizes divine beauty:
The face of God
Shining on us.

She does not do it because they oblige her.
She does not help him because he is family.
She does it.
That's all.
That's enough for her.

Wonderful, gentle Veronica.
There where we stretch our hands
Our eyes meet and our hearts talk.

Good, sensitive Veronica.
Where you are, is God.
You are your hand.
You are the hand of God.

During a few contemplative moments,
I pray, let go . . .

> Breathing in: *Just as you did it to one of these . . .*
> Breathing out: *. . . you did it to me.* (Matt 25:40)

God,
Shining face in Your Son,
Hidden for the world,
Also today You shine in many people.

Awaken in us Your Spirit so that
From now on, we are not blind to pain
And stretch out a hand to serve and love.

DRUCK

GEDEMÜTIGT

7

FIDELITY
Jesus meets his Father

The enemy behaves as a captain and chief of the army:
Where he finds us weakest [. . .], there he attacks us. [SpEx 327]

READINGS: Heb 5:7-10; Pss 4; 13; 22
EXERCISES: Meditation on sins [SpEx 45–54]
MUSIC: Marc-Antoine Charpentier (1643–1704), *Tenebrae factae sunt*,
   from *Leçons de ténèbres: Office du Jeudi Saint*

Jesus falls
Under the pressure of the cross.

It is a burden too hard to bear.

His face is turned towards heaven.

> How long, o Lord? Will you forget me forever?
> How long will you hide your face from me? (Ps 13:1)

Is this not a fourth encounter on the Way of the Cross?

> Answer me, o Lord, for your steadfast love is good;
> According to your abundant mercy, turn to me.
> Do not hide your face from your servant,
> For I am in distress—make haste to answer me.
> (Ps 69:16-17)

His hand falls open as an open question:

> My God, my God, why have you forsaken me? (Ps 22:1)

Without the light in your face
I cannot live.

What will get me up in the morning?
Not an idea, nor a habit.
It will be an encounter.
It will be the light in your eyes.

Here is all the humiliation of the world:
In his face, laid open towards the heavens.
There is all the despair of our world:
In his hand, laid open towards us.

Shall his hand find my hand?
Will this hand be filled again?

With his other hand, he grasps his cross.
His feet attempt—in vain—to stand again.
He is already standing up.
Faithful to his mission.
Faithful to his Father.
Faithful to us.

This is the Way of the Cross.
This is Jesus' way.
This is the Way:
Do not clasp your fists
But open your hand;
Do not bury yourself in your wounds
But ask for help.

Strength does not show itself
In the fear to fall
But in how and when one stands up again.

> There will be more joy in heaven
> Over one sinner who repents
> Than over ninety-nine righteous persons
> Who need no repentance. (Luke 15:7)

Even fallen, Jesus is the Rabbi, the Master.
He teaches me how to fall,
How to stand up,
How to go my way.

The Way of the Cross did not stop.
This is the way.
The only Way.

Under too much pressure,
We would close our hands,
Remain in bed,
And never stand again.

What gets me up in the morning?

Who gets me up in the morning?

> Give light to my eyes,
> Or I will sleep the sleep of death. (Ps 13:3)

Nothing is more practical than finding God,
That is, than falling in love in a quite absolute, final way.
What you are in love with, what seizes your imagination
Will affect everything.
It will decide what will get you out of bed in the mornings,
What you will do with your evenings,
How you spend your weekends,
What you read, who you know,
What breaks your heart, and what amazes you with joy and
    gratitude.
Fall in love, stay in love, and it will decide everything.

Pedro Arrupe, SJ

During a few contemplative moments,
I pray, let go . . .

> Breathing in: *Here I am . . .*
> Breathing out: *. . . to do your will.* (Ps 40:7-8)

God,
Fallen to earth in Your Son,
Also today You light up your face.

Awaken in us Your Spirit so that
From now on, we do not despair
But lift up our eyes.

8

CONSOLATION
Jesus meets us

I call desolation all the contrary of consolation,
Such as darkness of soul, disturbance in it,
Movement to things low and earthly,
The unquiet of different agitations and temptations,
Moving to want of confidence, without hope, without love,
When one finds oneself all lazy, tepid, sad, and as if separated
from his Creator and Lord. [SpEx 317]

READINGS: Matt 23:37-39; Luke 23:27-31
EXERCISES: Meditation on hell [SpEx 65–71]
MUSIC: Antonio Caldara (1670–1736), *Voglio piangere*, from
  Maddalena ai piedi di Cristo

A great number of the people followed him,
And among them were women who were beating their
breasts and wailing for him. But Jesus turned to them
and said:
"Daughters of Jerusalem, do not weep for me,
but weep for yourselves and for your children."
(Luke 23:27-28)

Again, Jesus turns around.
Again, Jesus stretches out his hand.
Again, Jesus finds the strength to console.

For it is clear that he did not come to help angels,
But the descendants of Abraham. (Heb 2:16)

Angels do not need his hand . . .
Between the second and the third fall,
Jesus stretches out his hand to console the people.

Comfort, o comfort my people. (Isa 40:1)

In the midst of his desolation,
Christ finds the strength to console and comfort.

He stretched out his hand and touched him, saying:
"I do choose. Be made clean!" (Matt 8:3)

Look at these people:
They rather look like salt columns,
Petrified in their tears,
Caryatids with nothing to carry.
Rocks without life.
Refugees without home, without hope.
Victims without face, without name.
The ones we see each day, again and again.
Silently, beaten, they pass over our screens
And yet we do not see them anymore.
There is no end to these suffering lines of terror and misery.

Jesus turns around.

Here is the man . . .

. . . who turns around.
Only God can look like this: up and back at people.
He lets his hand and his face
Shine over these petrified people
Who bury their faces in their hands
And suffocate in sadness.

People of desolation.
They do not walk anymore.
They are just there. Waiting. Hanging in darkness.
Waiting for a Savior.
Who will come?
Will anyone wake up?

> They went and woke him up, saying:
> "Lord, save us! We are perishing!" (Matt 8:25)

Angels do not need his hand . . .

Desolation petrifies.
Contrary to Jesus, who steps forward,
These women are rooted on the spot,
Unable to move forward or backward.

Desolation impoverishes.
These women have lost all their elegance,
Their nobility, their singularity.

Desolation keeps us imprisoned.
We cannot move anymore.
Everything is blocked around us.
We are being blocked off.

Desolation makes us blind.
We cannot see the way anymore.
Wrapped in darkness.

Desolation melts together.

These three people are one in their solitude and their
    misery.
Lukewarm and undecided.

I know your
    works; you are
    neither cold nor
    hot. I wish that
    you were either
    cold or hot.
So, because you
    are lukewarm,
    and neither
    cold nor hot,
    I am about to
    spit you out of
    my mouth.
    (Rev 3:15-16)

Desolation sucks all humanity out of us.
Desolation spits us out.
We are left without hope.
Wrapped in solitude.

O Lord, please take my life from me,
For it is better for me to die than to live. (Jon 4:3)

Jesus frees one hand
To console, comfort, cure, caress.
Here I am, I am my hand.
I give myself to you.
You see: it is an empty hand.
I do not have more.
It is all I can give, for now.

True: this is all.
There is no way to give more.

> No one has greater love than this,
> To lay down one's life for one's friends.   (John 15:13)

Just a minute ago, Jesus had his hand open to the heavens
To collect the fresh dew of the Spirit.
He does not keep it for himself:
Here we see him giving his Spirit away.

He frees his hand
To free the oppressed.

> The Spirit of the Lord is upon me . . .
> . . . to let the oppressed go free. (Luke 4:18)

Here are two figures:
Desolation and consolation.
One blocked, the other on the way.
One weak, the other strong.
One paralyzed, the other dynamic.
One dying, the other energetic.
One dark, the other lucid.
One doubting, the other trustful.
One anxious, the other quiet, serene, calm.

I recognize both tendencies in myself.

Desolation roots itself in reasons
That are no reasons:
"You cannot do it."
"You should not do this."
This is not your cross.
This is not your way.
Who do you think you are?

No! says consolation.
No! says Jesus' hand.

Get behind me, Satan!
You are a stumbling block to me;
For you are setting your mind not on divine things
But on human things. (Matt 16:23)

Consolation carries its cross
And steps forward.
She does not know how.
She does not know where it will lead her.
But she goes.
Trusting that the road will lead her.

They are like sheep without shepherd.
Jesus shows us a way out of this.
The way. The only way.
A door out of this despair. (John 10:9)
The hand of God.

The hand of the Creator recreates.
The hand of the Doctor cures.
The hand of the Bridegroom caresses.

Jesus waves his hand.
Goodbye! he seems to say.
I am gone.
Soon you won't see me anymore.

It is to your advantage that I go away. (John 16:7)

During a few contemplative moments,
I pray, let go . . .

Breathing in: *God . . .*
Breathing out: *. . . be merciful.* (Luke 18:13)

God,
Consolation in Your Son,
Unrecognized in our world,
Also today You give us Your hand.

Awaken in us Your Spirit so that
From now on, we do not distrust
But console like You.

THIRD STEP

PASSION—FIVE MYSTERIES

In this third step, I follow Jesus in his Passion. Five mysteries are five spiritual exercises to grow in surrender, honesty, obedience, trust, and letting go. Jesus is still the Way who shows me the only way to go . . . I ask the Lord to share the same passion for this world.

Consider how the Divinity hides Itself,
That is, how It could destroy Its enemies and does not
    do it,
And how It leaves the most sacred Humanity to suffer
    so very cruelly. [SpEx 196]

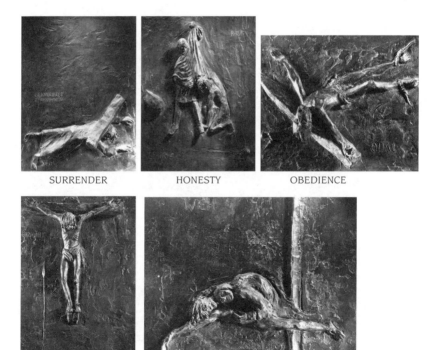

SURRENDER   HONESTY   OBEDIENCE

TRUST   LETTING GO

GEKNECHTET
ZERBROCHEN

9

SURRENDER

Jesus falls a last time

Let him who is in desolation consider how the Lord has left him
   in trial [. . .]
Since he can with the Divine help, which always remains to him,
Though he does not clearly perceive it. [SpEx 320]

READINGS: Phil 2:14-16; Mark 8:1-3; Matt 26:39
EXERCISES: Three ways of humility [SpEx 164–168]
MUSIC: Marc-Antoine Charpentier (1643–1704), *Miserere,* from
   Leçons de ténèbres: Office du Jeudi Saint

I am poured out like water,
And all my bones are out of joint.
My heart is like wax;
It is melted within my breast.
My mouth is dried up like a potsherd,
And my tongue sticks to my jaws;
You lay me in the dust of death. (Ps 22:14-15)

Two times I got up.
Not now. Not anymore.
Please. Let me die here.

I cannot do it. It is over.

It is enough now, o Lord,
Take away my life, for I am no better than my ancestors.
    (1 Kgs 19:4)

Poured out like water . . .
. . . you lay me in the dust of death.

I am a worm, and not human;
Scorned by others, and despised by the people. (Ps 22:6)

From here until he dies
Jesus will be alone.
Left alone.
No encounters anymore.
Totally pressed down, like the other one:

> A man was going down from Jerusalem to Jericho,
> And fell into the hands of robbers,
> Who stripped him, beat him, and went away,
> Leaving him half dead. (Luke 10:30)

By chance, a priest passes by.

> On the other side.

And a Levite.

> On the other side.

Who will be his Good Samaritan?
Who dares to walk on his side?

> I am a worm, and not human. (Ps 22:6)

Nobody is so human, so divine,
So open, so free, so humble.
The freedom and the humility
Of the few.

> He loved them to the end. (John 13:1)

This is his way to love us to the end.
This is the end.

Embracing the earth, dusting his body
In all the dust of the world,
He is moving mountains,
Breaking down walls.
He sets captives free
And sends the rich away empty, with open hands.

> I want and choose poverty with Christ poor rather than
> riches. [SpEx 167]

Poured out like water.
Open hands, open eyes, open mouth.
His whole humanity,
His whole divinity is poured out
In total surrender,
In everlasting sacrifice,
In utter freedom.
Crushed. Pulverized. Extended. Abandoned.

> All we like sheep have gone astray;
> We have all turned to our own way. (Isa 53:6)

Only he, the only Way,
Went the way nobody wanted to go.

During a few contemplative moments,
I pray, let go . . .

> Breathing in: *Not my will* . . .
> Breathing out: *. . . but yours.* (Luke 22:42)

God,
Delivered in Your Son,
Abandoned by all,
Also today You show us the way.

Awaken in us Your Spirit so that
From now on, we do not drift away
But walk with you.

10

HONESTY

Jesus is stripped of his clothes

When the enemy of human nature brings his wiles and
  persuasions to the just soul,
He wants and desires that they be received and kept in secret.
  [SpEx 326]

READINGS: Isa 53; Matt 13:44-46; John 19:23-24
EXERCISES: The call of the earthly king [SpEx 91–98]
MUSIC: Arvo Pärt (°1935), *Agnus Dei*, from *Missa sillabica*

Like a lamb that is led to the slaughter,
And like a sheep that before its shearers is silent,
So he did not open his mouth. (Isa 53:7)

From now on,
Jesus is manipulated like a lamb.

I can count all my bones.
They stare and gloat over me;
They divide my clothes among themselves,
And for my clothing they cast lots. (Ps 22:17-18)

They take off his clothes.
They take off his dignity.
As they still do with so many women, children, and men.

Homo ludens.
It's only a game.
It's only entertainment.
They are playing with their lives!

They laugh at his nudity.
They make fun of his vulnerability.
They dishonor the humanity they share.

Here is the man! (John 19:5)

Naked, like you and me.
Vulnerable, like us.
Flesh, loved by God.

Then the eyes of both were opened,
And they knew that they were naked. (Gen 3:7)

Naked, he came into the world.
Naked, he will go from here.

He, who never wore anything fancy,
Lets himself being stripped.

Now he resembles Adam.
He is the new Adam.

The strong one, clothed and with his hand in the air,
Is weak.
He hides himself behind Jesus' tunic.
He is the naked one.

> I was afraid, because I was naked;
> And I hid myself. (Gen 3:10)

His fist grasps, holds, does not let go.
It's mine! Here! Now!
At all costs.
At your cost.

> He had no form or majesty that we should look at him,
> Nothing in his appearance that we should desire him.
> He was despised and rejected by others;
> A man of suffering and acquainted with infirmity;
> And as one from whom others hide their faces. (Isa 53:3)

The soldier hides his face.
His mouth is covered.
He cannot utter a word.

The only word we hear is the Word of God,
Poor, naked, and dumb.

The weak one, naked and kneeling,
Is the strongest.
He shows a way out of this.
The way.
The only truth.
Life as it is.

The other is but a lie, a
disguise.
He has lost the innocence
of a child
—like us—
But with one difference:
He does not know how to
recover it!

To whom has the arm of the Lord been revealed? (Isa 53:1)

The arm of the Lord,
Not the arm of the soldier,
Protects and blesses:

This is my Son, the Beloved;
With him I am well pleased; listen to him! (Matt 17:5)

Jesus, the transfigured one,
Jesus, the disfigured one,
Kneels down.
Before all human misery.

Before our lie that does not know how to be transparent!
Before our hypocrisy that does not know how to be sincere!
Before our avarice that does not know how to give!

> YHWH God made garments of skin for Adam and for
>   his wife,
> And clothed them. (Gen 3:21)

> I was naked,
> And you did not give me clothing. (Matt 25:43)

During a few contemplative moments,
I pray, let go . . .

> Breathing in: *I believe . . .*
> Breathing out: *. . . help my unbelief!* (Mark 9:24)

God,
Silence in Your Son,
Silenced in our world,
Also today Your Word is poor, naked, and dumb.

Awaken in us Your Spirit so that
From now on, we do not steal anyone's dignity
But clothe ourselves with You.

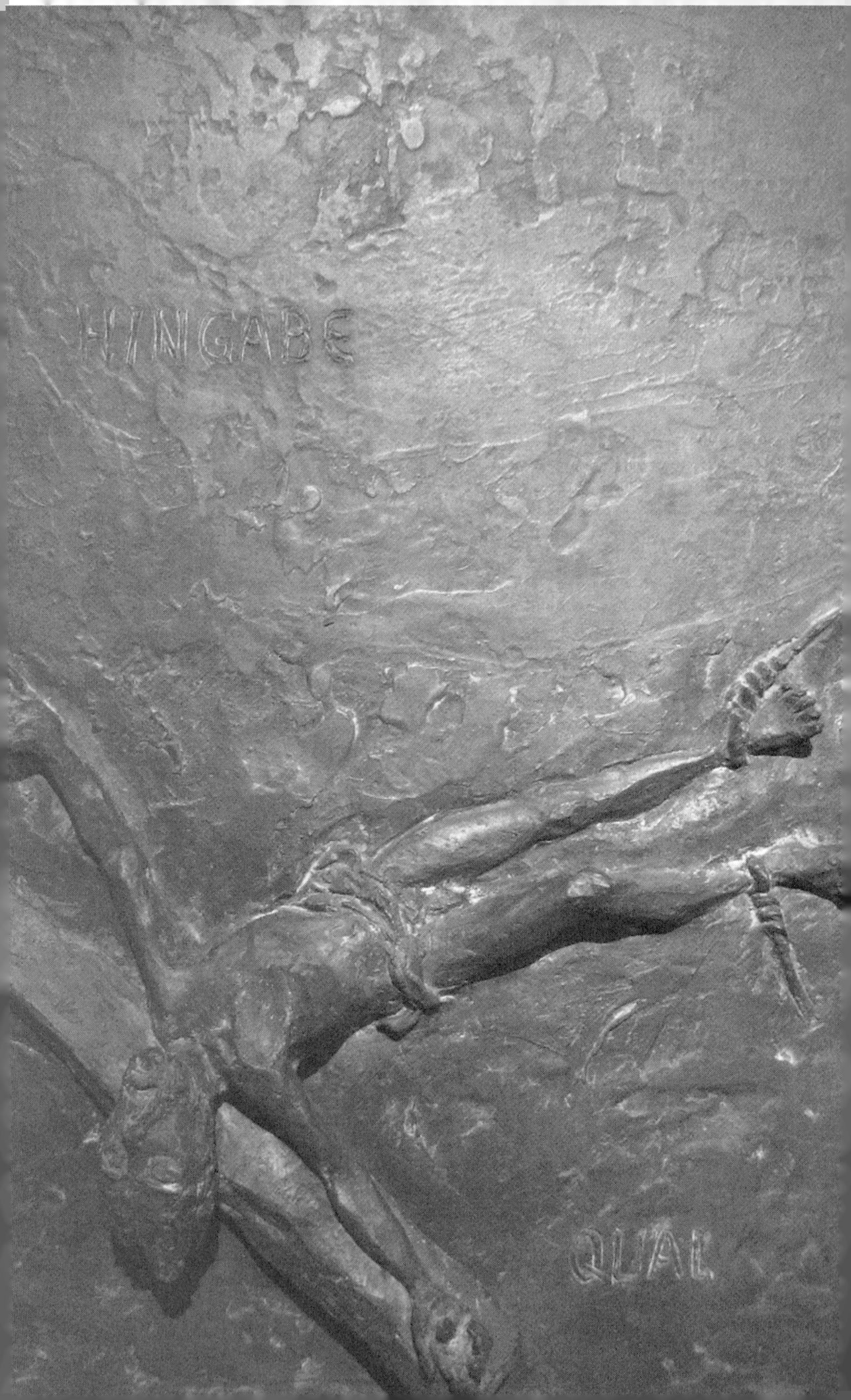
HINGABE
QUAL

11

OBEDIENCE
Jesus is nailed on the cross

It helps the person who was tempted by the enemy of human
    nature,
To look immediately at the course of the good thoughts which
    he brought him at their beginning [. . .]; in order that with
    this experience, known and noted, the person may be able
    to guard for the future against his usual deceits. [SpEx 334]

READINGS: Luke 23:33-43; John 19:18-24
EXERCISES: The first way of making an election [SpEx 179–183]
MUSIC: Marc-Antoine Charpentier (1643–1704), *Jerusalem surge*,
    from *Leçons de ténèbres: Office du Vendredi Saint*

Here is the man . . . (John 19:5)

. . . wounded for our transgressions,
crushed for our iniquities;
upon him was the punishment that made us whole,
and by his bruises we are healed. (Isa 53:5)

Here is a Transfiguration
So different from Mount Tabor.

This Golgotha Transfiguration
Is really a Disfiguration.

Suddenly there appeared to them Moses and Elijah,
Talking with him. (Matt 17:3)

Here, on Golgotha,
Nobody appears to converse with him.

So marred was his appearance, beyond human
semblance,
And his form beyond that of mortals. (Isa 52:14)

His real figure disappears from the face of the earth.
This transfiguration is much more common.
That is why it is so difficult to recognize God.

Whoever has seen me has seen the Father. (John 14:9)

Why is it so easy to disfigure the humanity we all share?
I see this disfiguration in the refugees, the prisoners, the
sick.
In the corners, in the streets, and in the gutters.
On the threshold between you and me.

Jesus is dumped in a corner,
Under a great void.

My God, my God, why have you forsaken me? (Ps 22:1)

He has still one hand free, not yet crucified,
That he lifts up to You:

Why, o why?

His head is totally torn towards the dark sky:

> Help me.

The Word in dialogue with Silence.
Nobody comes to help him.
His favorite friends have fled.
The leaders mock him:

> Let him save himself if he is the Messiah of God,
> His chosen one! (Luke 23:35)

It is so easy to mock a disfigured person!
This resembles the temptations in the desert:

> If you are the Son of God,
> Throw yourself down. (Matt 4:6)

Jesus does not follow their logic.
He is one with the crushed and crucified of our earth,
The victims, the forgotten ones.

The world upside down.
That is what he looks at, now, so turned and torn apart.

I look at his feet:
The Word of God has been captured
Like an animal.

> Like a lamb that is led to the slaughter. (Isa 53:7)

Here is the lamb that will save the sheep:

> All we like sheep have gone astray;
> We have all turned to our own way,
> And the Lord has laid on him
> The iniquity of us all. (Isa 53:6)

The Word of God has been silenced.

This is the heir;
Come, let us kill him and get his inheritance. (Matt 21:38)

We will recognize him at his hands and feet:

Look at my hands and my feet; see that it is I myself.
(Luke 24:39)

We will recognize him in his hands:

Put your finger here and see my hands.
Reach out your hand and put it in my side.
Do not doubt but believe. (John 20:27)

They will recognize us by our wounds.

There is nobody else with him.
He is left alone. Abandoned.
There is no point in condemning the executioners.
They do not have names; we do not see their faces.
That is not the point here.
They have already been forgiven

For they do not know what they are doing. (Luke 23:34)

During a few
contemplative
moments,
I pray, let go . . .

Breathing in: *Speak Lord . . .*
Breathing out: *. . . your servant is listening.* (1 Sam 3:9)

God,
Nailed through hands and feet in Your Son,
Pierced by our rebellion,
Also today You open Paradise for us.

Awaken in us Your Spirit
So that we do not point the finger at others
But, from now on, give them a hand.

ERHÖHT

SPOTT

12

TRUST

Jesus gives his Spirit

It is very helpful intensely to change ourselves against the
desolation,
As by insisting more on prayer, meditation, on much examination,
And by giving ourselves more scope in some suitable way of
doing penance. [SpEx 319]

READINGS: Matt 27:45-54; Mark 15:33-39; Ps 22
EXERCISES: Contemplation from Betania until the last supper
[SpEx 190–199]
MUSIC: Johann Sebastian Bach (1685–1750), *O süßes Kreuz*, from
Matthäus Passion

> Then Jesus, crying with a loud voice, said:
> "Father, into Your hands I commend my spirit."
> Having said this, He breathed his last.
>
> When the centurion saw what had taken place,
> He praised God and said:
> "Certainly this man was innocent." (Luke 23:46-47)

Also here He is alone.

In the hour of our death we die alone,
Even though surrounded by the ones we love.

His mouth falls open:

> It is finished.

His head falls.
He falls in the hands of the Father.
Completely surrendered.
Entirely mocked.

He is nothing.
He is finished.
He has nothing more to say,
Nothing more to do.

> Then He bowed His head and gave up His Spirit.
> (John 19:30)

Here is the man.

There he hangs,
To be mocked by us.

Spit on Him.
Despise Him.

> Away with him! Away with him! (John 19:15)

Poor King nailed on His throne of glory
Rich fruit hanging from the Tree of Life,
Leaning over towards us.

> Though He was rich, for your sakes He became poor,
> So that by His poverty you might become rich. (2 Cor 8:9)

No serpent on this tree (Gen 3:1-7).
Only a Fruit to be enjoyed.
You will not die by eating this Fruit (Gen 3:3).
You will certainly live.

> Bear much fruit.
> That your joy may be complete. (John 15:5, 11)

He bowed His head to the world
As the slave to the master
As the faithful to their God.

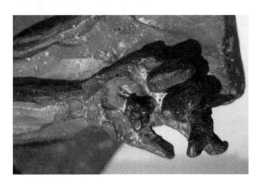

He bows His head to me
And opens His eyes
Searching for my eyes
His mouth falls open
Searching for my mouth

. . . what will I say to Him?

> Away with him! Away with him! (John 19:15)
>
> Certainly this man was innocent. (Luke 23:47)

This cup will not be removed from us (Luke 22:42):
This cup is freely offered to be drunk.

> Just as Moses lifted up the serpent in the wilderness,
> So must the Son of Man be lifted up. (John 3:14)

Look at Him.
Look Him in the eyes.

> When they look on the one whom they have pierced,
> They shall mourn for him, as one mourns for an only
>   child,
> And weep bitterly over him, as one weeps over a first-
>   born. (Zech 12:10)

Behold the Lamb of God,
Sacrificed for us.

Behold the Man of God
Who can save us.

> Certainly this man was innocent.

Innocent as so many women, men, and children
Who die today due to their innocent color, gender, race,
  religion, or orientation.

  Away with them! Away with them!

No one there to help them.
They die alone.

  Certainly they were innocent.
From now on, the Word of God is silenced.
The Light of the World is extinguished.

It is silent now,
Silent as the night.

  Certainly . . .

It is too late now.
It is night.

During a few contemplative moments,
I pray, let go . . .

  Breathing in: *Into your hands . . .*
  Breathing out: *. . . I commend my spirit.* (Luke 23:46)

God,
Silenced in Your Son,
Mistreated by our lack of concern,
Also today You give abundant life.

Awaken in us Your Spirit so that
From now on, we are not clinging onto ourselves
But carry fruit as the grain of wheat.

13

LETTING GO

Pieta: Jesus in the arms of his mother

Eternal Lord of all things, I make my oblation with your favor
and help,
In the presence of your infinite Goodness and in presence of
your glorious Mother
And of all the saints of the heavenly court; that I want and desire,
And it is my deliberate determination, if only it be for your greater
service and praise,
To imitate you in bearing all injuries and all abuse and all
poverty of spirit,
And actual poverty, too,
If your most Holy Majesty wants to choose and receive me to
such life and state. [SpEx 98]

READINGS: Matt 27:55-58; Mark 15:40-46; Ps 71
EXERCISES: Contemplation of the entire Passion [SpEx 208–209]
MUSIC: Giovanni Pierluigi da Palestrina (1525–1594), *Stabat Mater*

> When evening had come, and since it was the day of
>   Preparation,
> That is, the day before the sabbath, Joseph of Arimathea,
> A respected member of the council, who was also him-
>   self waiting expectantly for the kingdom of God, went
>   boldly to Pilate and asked for the body of Jesus. (Mark
>   15:42-43)

Often it is so busy under the cross:
We see Joseph of Arimathea and Nicodemus,
John and Mary,
And an entire group of women (Matt 27:56).

Here, we only see Mary
Curved over her dead son.

No polished pieta,
Purely presented to our marvelous meditation.

No: just a mother
Entirely surrendered to her sorrow, to her son.

Even better: the most human of mothers
Totally handed over to the most human of sons
In the most human of sorrows.

Curved,
        curled,
                clinched,
                        coiled,

yes, clothed in one last embrace.

Turned,
        twisted,
                entwined,
                        entangled,
                                interwoven

in the fabric of her son.

As if to clothe Him,
To be his last garment.
As if to take Him in,
One last time,
One last hug.
This she had done all her life:
Giving Him birth
Carrying Him through life
Bending over to Him.

This defined who she was
This defined who she wanted to be:
A tremendous capacity of empathy.

It was dark.

May I take You in my arms,
One last time?
I want to caress You,
With my whole heart,
With my whole body,
With my whole being.

My heart upon Your heart
I want to warm Your heart.

> Were not our hearts burning within us
> While He was talking to us on the road? (Luke 24:31)

Now Mary lays emptied, liquefied, poured out
Over her dead body.

> I am poured out like water,
> And all my bones are out of joint;
> My heart is like wax;
> It is melted within my breast.
> My mouth is dried up like a potsherd,
> And my tongue sticks to my jaws;
> You lay me in the dust of death. (Ps 22:14-15)

She lays down on Him,
As to give Him that last bit of warmth.
Tenderly, her hand is a small bowl
To staunch the wound
To collect the blood
A chalice of life, her hand
That just a minute ago softly caressed his cheek.

Bent,
    bowed,
        stretched,
            unfolded,
                opened up

As to identify herself with her Son.

She does not remain safely at a distance
She dares to surrender herself
In one pure curl of love.

Bleeding open,
She prefers the curve of love
To the straight line of the bodice
And the disdaining lips.

Stretched upon her son
Just as the prophet Elijah
Raised the dead son of a widow (1 Kgs 17:21).

Stretched upon her son
Just as God created Adam from dust (Gen 2:7).

In this way, God stamped us with Spirit,
Image and resemblance (Gen 1:26).

In this way, we become able to love
Each other, but also God;
God, but also each other.

Tenderly, she holds Him
Not to oppress or suppress
But to impress Him in her heart:
Soft imprint that expressly begs
For a new impression

   . . . to treasure in her heart. (Luke 2:51)

Dare to say your love
With your body.

   Noli me tangere.
   Do not hold on to Me. (John 20:17)

To hold is allowed here,
In this eternal moment of intimate goodbye.

This is her way of letting go.

She does not clamp herself to Him;
She does not desperately attempt to protect Him.

She knows very well that it is good for Him to leave.

   It is to your advantage that I go away,
   For if I do not go away, the Advocate will not come to
   you. (John 16:7)

And yet, the pain cuts deep.
Love does not take away pain,
On the contrary.

> The days will come when the bridegroom is taken
>   away from then,
> And then they will fast on that day. (Mark 2:20)

The Mother of God
Expresses here in her body
The surrender of God the Father to the Son,
In the Spirit.

One could say: between these two,
Mother and Son,
There is no space anymore.

Together they form new space,
A new form of Space,
The Godspace of the Spirit.
Together they are Body, they are Spirit.
And for now, this Spirit is surrendered to pain and sorrow.

For now, sorrow is allowed.
Now is the time for grieving.
This grieving expresses my love.
This grieving *is a fast in which the Lord delights*
    (Isa 58:1-14).

In the worst of my miseries I keep trusting in the Lord.

> Though the fig tree does not blossom,
> And no fruit is on the vines;
> Though the produce of the olive fails
> And the fields yield no food;
> Though the flock is cut off from the fold
> And there is no herd in the stalls,
> Yet I will rejoice in the Lord;
> I will exult in the God of my salvation. (Hab 3:17-18)

Here is the man . . .

. . . at the foot of the cross,
That ghastly, grisly line in the night,
That only sharpens how lifeless they lie there,
Poured out in the dust of the world.

Death was stronger.
Death killed them,
Mother and Son,
God and Man.

> . . . but we had hoped that he was the one to redeem
> Israel! (Luke 24:21)

And yet, this encounter is entirely clothed in empty silence,
breathtaking,
breathing
still life
empty silence
for breathing—
the breath of the Spirit.

The pulse lifts her body barely noticeable
In soft, gentle gasps
The only warmth,
The only breathing heart
The only human shape
In cold metallic infinity.

An audaciously empty flatness,
Stilled mist
Leaving barely visible
Hardly human bodies
Held in the exclamation to heaven.

Announced here are the
Depth and height of Holy Saturday,
Unfathomable divine sorrow.

. . . we are facing God's own wound of love.

The cross is now Tree of Life
Bridging heaven and earth,
Deeply rooted in human and divine suffering.

Even though people have fallen deep in death,
God can raise them up from that depth,
Because Godself went that way.

The right hand of Jesus
Loosely points to that depth,
That sheol that holds us in death,
That darkness that keeps me enslaved
In but desiring shades.
From myself I cannot climb out of that dark pit.

The agile hand of our ultimate Judge
Reminds us of such abysmal sin,
Such bottomless depth,
Such fathomless death,
This hell that also today
Suffocates men, women, and children
In its deathly, impure embrace.

Delicately that light hand points
To such an atrocious scene in the dark—
Lowliness unworthy of being sculpted,
Unnecessary to be imagined,
For it is daily news
That is never new.

The Good News of the Gospel
Is that Jesus does not abandon us.

Who closely observes
Can see His silent smile.

He passed away smiling.

Who patiently waits
Can hear His laughter.

He, the Good Judge,
The Good Shepherd,
Does not leave alone any lost lamb (Luke 15; John 10).

That hand, loosely letting go,
Is the same as just a minute ago,
Calling me in
Calling me to follow Him
On his way.

> This is the way that I must go.
> This is the Way of the Cross that I must go
>   (Mark 8:31-33).

This hand is the one calling Adam out of his death
The one calling Matthew out of his death
Calling the two Simons out of their death
Calling me
Like he called the centurion:

> Truly this man was God's Son! (Matt 27:54)

Even His death is vocation,
Invocation, convocation
Provocation to follow Him.

Ah! Would all start to believe in Him!
The world would be opened to them.

Curled over her Son,
Mary follows His line,
The line that points towards the depths.
She becomes one with that line,
With that last Word of God.

Mary is no obstacle to that Word,
She allows it to be heard.

Mary, the human amplifier of that divine Word,
Who *proclaims it from the housetops* (Matt 10:27).

Magnificat

My soul magnifies the Lord. (Luke 1:46)

Lying down, stretching out on her Son,
Mary becomes His Yes to the Father.

Fiat

Here I am, the servant of the Lord;
Let it be with me according to your word. (Luke 1:38)

The open wound is opened to us.
Even dead, He continues to give Himself to us.
It is the wound of the heart,
The wound of love.

With her hand,
Chalice of life,
Mary becomes this wound,
She *is* this wound.

Bone of my bones,
Flesh of my flesh. (Gen 2:23)

It is also *her* wound,
Continuously overflowing graces.
She recognizes herself in this wound.

In reality, this whole scene is but one open wound,
God's open wound of love
Surrendered to our world
Today.

Mary, Mother of God,
Softly whispers in my ear:

Do not be afraid to love,
For God is love.

During a few contemplative moments,
I pray, let go . . .

    Breathing in: *O that today . . .*
    Breathing out: . . . *you would listen to his voice!*
    (Ps 95:7)

God,
Invisible wound of love in Your dead Son,
Deceased due to our malevolence,
Also today You live and suffer under our indifference.

Awaken in us Your Spirit so that
From now on, we are not afraid of your
unfathomable love
But surrender ourselves, like Mary intimate and near.

FOURTH STEP

LIFE—TWO VIRTUES

PATIENCE

JOY

Consider how God works and labors for me
In all things created on the face of the earth. [SpEx 236]

This fourth step invites us to contemplate the effects of the resurrection in our world today. Two virtues are especially apt as spiritual exercises in this world: patience and joy. Jesus shows us how to go this way. It is in this world that God continues to work and labor for his Kingdom. Instead of a superficial optimism, Jesus invites us to a joy rooted in the unending source of love and hope, God. It could be so that the intensity of our joy is correlated to the density of our patience, the depth of our passion.

VERLOREN

14

PATIENCE
Jesus entombed

Let him who is in desolation labor to be in patience. [SpEx 321]

READINGS: Mark 15:42-47; John 19:38-42; Ps 22
EXERCISES: The election [SpEx 184–187]
MUSIC: Arvo Pärt (°1935), *Passio*

Joseph took the body and wrapped it in a clean linen cloth
And laid it in his own new tomb, which he had hewn in the
    rock. He then rolled a great stone to the door of the tomb
    and went away.
Mary Magdalene and the other Mary were there,
Sitting opposite the tomb. (Matt 27:59-61)

Still, Jesus lets Himself be manipulated.
He lets Himself be laid in the tomb.

And then everything became silent, really silent.
Everything was wrapped up in silence: mute, speechless
    stillness.
A Holy, wordless Saturday without end.
The Word of God has been silenced.
As it happens every day.

Was it but a dream?

    . . . but we had hoped that he was the one to redeem
      Israel! (Luke 24:21)

Will this silence be able to redeem us?
Will new life break out of this tomb?
Will it ever dawn on us?

For the first time
We do not witness people anymore,
Only a dark, closed gate,
A hard stone that no one is able to roll away.
A thick wall that no one is able to break down.

It blocks my view,
My vision, my dream, my hope.

The gate is closed,
Nobody can continue this way.

    The gate to Paradise is forever shut,
      Nobody can get in.

    The gate of Sheol is shut,
      Nobody can get out.

The sheep are *without a shepherd* (Matt 9:36);
No gate that stands open for them

No gate that goes open for them,
No gate *that lays down his life for the sheep* (John 10:7-11).

One word is carved into the stone:

> *Verloren*—Lost.

Yes, He is lost in death.
Yes, we are lost in death.

That round stone is like a mirror
That reflects my own face,
That hard metallic mask of Pilate
That is so often my own dark mask
Occulting and scrupulously protecting my own treasure,
my own nothingness,
my own tomb.

A closed tomb?
. . . it is not an image in which I want to be reflected.

During a few contemplative moments,
I pray, let go . . .

> Breathing in: *Speak Lord . . .*
> Breathing out: *. . . your servant is listening.* (1 Sam 3:9)

God,
Lost in Your Son,
Excluded out of our lives,
Also today You do not rule Yourself out.

Awaken in us Your Spirit
So that, from now on, we do not exclude ourselves
from Your life
But rather await You with hope.

15

JOY

Jesus rises

It is the property of the Creator to enter, go out and cause
  movements in the soul,
Bringing it all into love of His Divine Majesty. [SpEx 330]

READINGS: John 20:11-18; Luke 24:13-35
EXERCISES: Contemplation to attain love [SpEx 230–237]
MUSIC: Georg Frideric Händel (1685–1759), *Hallelujah,* from *The
  Messiah*

All of a sudden, bronze breaks open.

Unexpectedly, He breaks out.
Swiftly, an awakened God wakes us
Out of our eternal sleep.

Then their eyes were opened,
And they recognized Him. (Luke 24:31)

Suddenly, He breaks through our death,
Through all that maintains us
blocked,
   concealed,
     covered,
       buried,
         folded,
           obscured,
             excluded,
              expelled,
               suppressed,
              detached,
               isolated,
                desolate
solely focused upon ourselves.

He unfolds, again and again, all those unnecessary folds,
All those *wrappings lying there* (John 20:6)
In one simple fold—untold,
   one
      single
        never-ending
          unraveling
            movement
              onto the open.

A smile . . .
and there was light. (Gen 1:3)

. . . He called Mary by her name. (John 20:16)

Listen: He keeps on calling.

He keeps on calling us.
By our name.

Even today.

> She turned around and said to Him: Rabbouni!
>   (John 20:16)

There He stands,
As if on the prow of a ship,
The ship of His Church in the world,
That chaste prostitute, *casta meretrix*,
That poor holy human Church,
Where even today His Spirit blows,
Like *the wind blows where it chooses,*
Without us knowing *where it comes from or where it goes.*
   (John 3:8)

There He stands,
Continuously blowing the Church open from within,
                    towards the world,
                    towards the future.

With the same
        swelling force,
        blowing wind,
        unstoppable enthusiasm
            of the creating,
                    healing,
                        sanctifying Spirit who makes
                                whole
                holy   whole   holy
                        whole
                        what is broken.

There He opens
With lofty hand
The soaring doors of death.

There He abandons
With wide-open eyes
The bronze era that turns us into stone.

There He dives
Through the golden waves of the Spirit
Into the wide-open sky.

There He drinks
With overflowing gulps
The fresh air of the Spirit.

There He dances
With young, healthy cheeks
The unending circle of life.

There He rises:
A new Sun in the East,
A new Son in the Orient,
Who orients,
>   brightens,
>>   warms our world.

During a few contemplative moments,
I pray, let go . . .

> Breathing in: *Yes, Lord . . .*
> Breathing out: *. . . you know that I love you.*
>   (John 21:15)

God,
Swelling force in Your Son,
Broken by our night,
Also today You break through like the dawn.

Awaken in us Your Spirit
So that, from now on, we live simply unfolded
Oriented towards the One who is to come.

Music Suggestions

J. S. Bach, *Matthäus Passion*
Philippe Herreweghe (Harmonia Mundi 2003) HMX 2901155.57

J. S. Bach, *Johannes Passion*
Philippe Herreweghe (Harmonia Mundi 1988) HMC 1264.65

A. Caldara, *Maddalena ai piedi di Cristo*
René Jacobs (Harmonia Mundi 2002) HMC 905221.22

M.-A. Charpentier, *Leçons de ténèbres. Office du Jeudi Saint*
Il seminario musicale, Veritas (Virgin Classics 1995) VC 5 45075 2

M.-A. Charpentier, *Leçons de ténèbres. Office du Vendredi Saint*
Il seminario musicale, Veritas (Virgin Classics 1993) VC 7 59295 2

F. Couperin, *Leçons de ténèbres*
Deller, Todd, Chapuis (Harmonia Mundi 2001) HMA 195210

G. Fauré, *Requiem*
Schola Cantorum Oxford (Naxos 1994) 8.550765

La divine liturgie de Saint-Jean Chrysostome
Dimitre Rouskov (Harmonia Mundi 1976) HMC 90641

G. F. Händel, *Utrecht Te Deum*
Simon Preston, L'Oiseau-Lyre (Decca 1994) 443 178-2

A. Pärt, *Missa Sillabica*
Paul Hillier (Harmonia Mundi 1999) HMX 2957182

A. Pärt, *Passio*
The Hilliard Ensemble (ECM 1988) ECM 1370837 109-2